Kathy Burke

MR THOMAS

NICK HERN BOOKS

London

www.nickhernbooks.co.uk

A Nick Hern Book

This revised edition of *Mr Thomas* first published in Great Britain as a paperback original in 2017 by Nick Hern Books Limited, The Glasshouse, 49a Goldhawk Road, London W12 8QP

First published by Nick Hern Books in *First Run 3* in 1991

Cover image: original Old Red Lion poster artwork and Shutterstock/Nadezhda Bolotina

Designed and typeset by Nick Hern Books, London
Printed in the UK by Mimeo Ltd, Huntingdon, Cambridgeshire PE29 6XX

A CIP catalogue record for this book is available from the British Library

ISBN 978 1 84842 649 8

Introduction
Kathy Burke

In the mid- to late 1980s I was a young character actress. I had a few nice jobs under my belt, but most of the stuff I was doing was very samey and the 'resting' in-between was getting on my nerves. I decided to get more involved. I produced and assistant-directed *Therapy* by Robert Pugh at the Old Red Lion Pub Theatre and then, when Ken McClymont became Artistic Director there, I would help him read through the piles of new plays that were sent on a weekly basis, whilst also working behind the bar of the pub for cigarette money.

Apart from the odd freebie, the only theatre I could afford to see was on the fringe, so my love for Wilde, Coward, Pinter and Orton came from reading their work or seeing film/TV adaptations.

Because of my love at the time for these masters I was fascinated by repressed sexuality, alcoholism, bedsit land and murder, so I decided to write a play. I purposely didn't include a character I could play myself (I was too young for Mrs Tebbit and now, thankfully, I am too old). I wanted better acting roles, of course, but felt I had to show that I could understand and empathise with characters other than short, fat girls with a love for doughnuts.

It took a few years after first writing to pluck up the courage to do a rehearsed reading. Amongst the invited audience were people who I knew were relatively rich, in the hope that I could raise some funds from here and there to put the play on, and the actor/writer/director Philip Davis who, if I got the money, I wanted as the play's director.

It went down a storm. One of my rich friends, Simon Brint, came straight up to me after, asked how much was needed, then immediately and extremely generously said he would give me all of the money – so the begging bowl was put away. Phil Davis joined us, was exuberant about the play but said, 'I'm not going to direct it though as I think you should direct it yourself.' And Simon, who was now my producer said, 'I couldn't agree more.' So that was that.

We started rehearsals in January 1990. I had a great time, one of the happiest and most rewarding of my career. After a quiet opening, word of mouth and (mostly) favourable reviews (my favourite of which included 'Miss Burke's use of language would shock a docker!') led to a sell-out audience for three of its four-week run.

A few months later it won a Time Out Theatre Award; a few months after that it was televised by Channel 4 as part of its Small Stages season with established director Herbie Wise (*I, Claudius*) taking the helm; and a few months after that it was published by Nick Hern Books in *First Run 3*. It was all very exciting and beautifully uplifting.

I didn't fall in love with writing as it's too lonely and really bloody hard, but it kicked off my passion for directing and it did lead to much better acting roles. Job done.

January 2017

Mr Thomas was first performed at the Old Red Lion Theatre, London, on 30 January 1990, with the following cast:

GEORGE	James Clyde
WEAVER	Ray Winstone
GORDON	Oliver Smith
MRS TEBBIT	Anita Graham
MR THOMAS	Ian Jentle
Director	Kathy Burke
Designers	Matthew Duguid
	John Pope
Producer	Simon Brint

For John and Barry

Characters

GEORGE, *mid- to late twenties. Not very healthy looking but has an attractive face. Quiet personality.*

WEAVER, *late thirties. Small and stocky. Scruffy in appearance, flash and sure of himself. A pain in the bum.*

MRS TEBBIT, *mid-forties. Dowdy one minute, stunning the next. Frustrated in every way.*

GORDON, *late forties. Smart dresser, upper-class, the ex-army type.*

THOMAS, *late forties to early fifties. Small and weak, a nervous wreck. Wears glasses.*

The play takes place one day in a small bedsit in London, some time in the late 1950s.

ACT ONE

Scene One

Setting: the attic room of a house. A bed in one corner, a battered armchair in another. A sink with a mishmash of pots, plates and cups. A portable record player and discs scattered around it. Damp-ridden walls, old lino covers the floor. The curtains are always closed and the room is lit by a large floor lamp. The door to the room is upstage next to an old wardrobe. The whole room should give off a feeling of despair.

Morning. GEORGE is asleep on the bed on top of the covers. He has slept in his clothes and they are a crumpled mess. There is a knock on the door. GEORGE doesn't move. After a pause another knock, this time louder.

WEAVER (*off*). George?... George? Are you awake?

GEORGE (*stirs slightly and looks up. Mumbles*). What?

WEAVER (*off*). George? Wake up. Come on, I know you're in.

GEORGE (*sits up*). Who is it?

WEAVER (*off*). ME.

GEORGE. Who?

WEAVER (*off*). Stop fucking about, George. It's me, Weaver, come on, let me in.

GEORGE. What do you want?

WEAVER. Just let us in, will you. Stop playing silly buggers.

GEORGE. Hold on a minute. (*Gets up, staggers to the door and opens it.*)

WEAVER (*entering*). Fuck me, it's freezing out there. I've just been up the dole, thought I'd pop in and see you as I was in the area. Hope you don't mind.

GEORGE (*goes to the sink and splashes his face with water*). Do you want a cup of tea?

WEAVER. Wouldn't mind.

GEORGE. I ain't got no milk though.

WEAVER. Oh. You got any coffee?

GEORGE. No.

WEAVER. I don't think I'll bother then. I'm not being rude or anything, it's just that I can't stand tea without milk. I can do without it in coffee but I have to have milk in tea even if it's just a splash.

GEORGE. Well I ain't got none, I'm afraid.

WEAVER. No worries. I didn't really fancy one anyway.

GEORGE. I've got a drop of whisky if you'd care for it.

WEAVER. Oh I dunno. Bit early ain't it?

GEORGE. It's twenty-to.

WEAVER. Is it?

GEORGE. I might be a bit slow.

WEAVER. Fuck it. The pubs are open in half an hour so it wouldn't be too out of order would it?

GEORGE (*gets the whisky from the wardrobe and pours out two generous amounts*). Do you want water in it?

WEAVER. Just a splash, don't go mad.

GEORGE. There you go.

WEAVER. Smashing. Just what the doctor ordered.

Pause.

GEORGE. What a night.

WEAVER. Rough was it?

GEORGE (*sits on the bed*). Murder. God knows how I got home.

WEAVER. That bad? I should've been there.

GEORGE. You would've loved it.

WEAVER. I had a gyppy tummy. Don't know what was the matter with me. I couldn't walk.

GEORGE. You alright now?

WEAVER. Kosher. I must've had a bug or something.

GEORGE. Well, you missed a good night.

WEAVER. It's always the way, ain't it. Life can be a bit of a bollock like that.

GEORGE. Not to worry. He's bound to have another one soon.

WEAVER. Who was there then?

GEORGE. Just the usual mob, plus a few I'd never met before. Nice people though, friendly.

WEAVER. Any women there?

GEORGE. Quite a few, as it goes.

WEAVER. Any salty ones?

GEORGE. One or two. That bird was there.

WEAVER. What bird?

GEORGE. That bird, you know.

WEAVER. What one?

GEORGE. The one with the teeth.

WEAVER. They've all got teeth, well, most of them have.

GEORGE. Yeah but she's got big ones, you know, sort of goofy but not goofy, goofy, if you know what I mean.

WEAVER. What colour hair?

GEORGE. Sort of blonde-ish, oh you know her but I can't remember her name.

WEAVER. Not Gloria?

GEORGE. No, I know Gloria, don't I. She's a bit plump, not fat, just a bit plump, fat arse.

WEAVER. Oh I know who you mean, that's what's-her-name, Janet!

GEORGE. Janet, that's it. She asked me where you were.

WEAVER. Yeah? What did you say?

GEORGE. I said you were at home with a bad tummy; she looked a bit put out.

WEAVER. Did she? Oh that's good. I quite like her.

GEORGE. She left with some bloke, though.

WEAVER. Did she? Who?

GEORGE. I don't know, one of Derek's mates.

WEAVER. What, was she with him then?

GEORGE. Well she didn't come with him, just left with him.

WEAVER. Yeah, she's a bit loose like that.

GEORGE. Is she?

WEAVER. Yeah. Puts it about a bit. Nice girl though.

GEORGE. She didn't look like she'd put it about.

WEAVER. Well she's not a slag or anything, she don't just go with anyone. I only know a couple of geezers that have had her.

GEORGE. Have you?

WEAVER. What?

GEORGE (*shyly*). You know.

WEAVER. Yeah, once or twice.

GEORGE. You sly bugger.

WEAVER. What?

GEORGE. You never told me.

WEAVER. Well I don't have to tell you do I?

GEORGE. No but...

WEAVER. I don't think I told anybody. I don't see why I should have to. I hate it when blokes mouth off about the birds they pull and all the ins and outs as to what they do with them. I respect women, I do. I mean you've got to respect them or they won't respect us.

GEORGE. Yeah, I suppose you're right.

WEAVER. I mean you never tell me about the birds you pull.

GEORGE. Well, no. I don't think it's something you should talk about.

WEAVER. Well that's my point, ain't it. You still ask me questions though, don't you.

GEORGE. Yeah I know... I shouldn't... It's not right. Sorry, Weaver.

WEAVER. No, don't apologise, George. You're my mate, you never have to say sorry to me, I was just making a point, that's all.

Pause.

Wish I'd gone last night, I'd like to see Janet again. Still, I'm bound to bump into her some time.

GEORGE. Well she did say she'd pop in The Crown one night.

WEAVER. Did she? When?

GEORGE. She didn't say.

WEAVER. Well that's a bugger, ain't it.

GEORGE. What is?

WEAVER. Well she could've said when. I mean, I might not be there.

GEORGE. Might not be there when?

WEAVER. When she pops in. The night she decides to pop into The Crown I might be somewhere else.

GEORGE. But you're always in The Crown. You don't go anywhere else.

WEAVER. I'm not always in there. I wasn't there last night.

GEORGE. That's because you had a gyppy tummy.

WEAVER. I know, but I still don't go there every night. We often go to The Swan for a change, don't we.

GEORGE. Only now and then. We're usually in The Crown.

WEAVER. I know that, that's not the point though is it? I mean, one night we might decide to go down The Swan, for a change sort of thing, and Janet might go down The Crown thinking I'd be in there because *you*, soppy bollocks, told her I'm in there all the time and forgot to mention the fact that every now and then we pop in The Swan.

GEORGE. Oh I see what you mean now.

WEAVER. See really, she should have told you a certain night so I could make sure I was in there. You see, George, some women just take it for granted that you're gonna be around when it's convenient for them. They don't think most of them. They're just all hair and legs.

Beat.

And what if she decided to pop in and I was with another bird, she wouldn't like that, would she?

GEORGE. No, I don't suppose she would.

WEAVER. So you can see what I'm getting at then?

GEORGE. Oh yeah.

Pause.

WEAVER. It's a bit cheeky when you think about it. Still, it's her loss… fat fucker! You got any more Scotch going?

GEORGE. Do you want some?

WEAVER. If you don't mind, if you've got any spare. I wouldn't want you to think I was poncing.

GEORGE (*pours out more drink*). Don't be silly. What's mine is yours. You're my mate.

WEAVER. You're a good bloke, George. No doubt about it, you're a little diamond.

GEORGE. Leave it out.

WEAVER. Don't be embarrassed. I mean it. A man couldn't ask for a finer friend.

GEORGE. Well it works both ways, you know.

WEAVER. You've got a point there. That's a bloody good point, George. I mean, I think you're a good bloke and I know you think I'm a good bloke, so we get on. We're sort of compatible, ain't we?

GEORGE. That's one way of looking at it.

WEAVER. No, mate. It's the only way to look at it. It may sound daft but it's as if we were made for each other. I don't mean in the way that men and women are made for each other, I mean in the way that men and men are made for each other, do you see what I mean?

GEORGE. Sort of.

WEAVER. How old are you?

GEORGE. Twenty-seven.

WEAVER. Is that all?

GEORGE. Yeah. Why, how old did you think I was?

WEAVER. Don't know, never really thought about it before, didn't think you was as young as that though. Still, you learn something new every day don't you? Anyway, back to my point. Now you've lived for twenty-seven years right?

GEORGE. Right.

WEAVER. Now in those twenty-seven years you must have had mates come and go, right?

GEORGE. Right.

WEAVER. Now me, I've lived for thirty-six years…

GEORGE. Are you thirty-six?

WEAVER. Yeah, surprising, ain't it. Now I've certainly seen a lot of mates come and go. Some have been alright and some have been right-bastards, but you, George, and I can say this in all honesty, you have been the best mate I've ever had. You see, the main base of a friendship is built on trust and I know I can trust you. I've told you a lot of things about myself and about other people and I've always known you wouldn't breathe a word of it to anyone.

GEORGE. Of course I wouldn't. It's only right, isn't it. I'd never betray someone else's confidence.

WEAVER. That's why you're my mate.

GEORGE. I trust you as well, you know.

WEAVER. Of course you do.

GEORGE. I've told you loads of things I wouldn't dream of telling anyone else.

WEAVER. That's right. I've got a lot on you, ain't I, George.

Pause.

This is the life, ain't it. Look at us aye, not a care in the world. I feel sorry for those poor buggers who have to go to work every day.

GEORGE. Silly ain't they.

WEAVER. No. I wouldn't call them silly, George; I think 'sad' is a more appropriate word. They don't know how to relax, see. Everything is one big rush to them, even when they're on their holidays. I've studied them down in Southend, I often study people, it's the intelligent man's pastime. What they do is they rush out of bed before all the hot water goes, then they rush down to breakfast before some fat bastard from Wigan eats the last of the bacon, then they rush down to the beach, rush back to the digs for dinner, rush out to the dance halls to have a quick jive before they have to rush back again in case the landlady locks them out all night. It's a fucking joke! Give me this life any time. Every day's a holiday ain't it. I mean, I know we ain't got as much money as them, but who needs it, that's what I'd like to know.

GEORGE. Well if you ever do go short you know you can always come to me for a bob or two, and vice versa I suppose.

WEAVER. Exactly. You've just taken the words right out of my mouth.

Pause.

Yep, it's all a waste of time, work and families and that, all one big waste of space.

GEORGE. I wouldn't mind a couple of kids one day; I know it sounds silly but I've got a bit of a soft spot for them.

WEAVER. Yeah, but to have kids you need a wife, don't you, George.

GEORGE. Well I wouldn't mind getting married one day either.

WEAVER. Oh leave it out, I know for a fact you're not the marrying kind.

GEORGE. Ain't I?

WEAVER. Of course you ain't, you like your freedom too much, don't you.

GEORGE. Well I do now, but I might change my mind in a couple of years and want to settle down.

WEAVER. You've got to get a job if you want to settle down.

GEORGE. But what I'm saying is, I might change. I mean, I know that right now the last thing I want is a job and a wife and that, but you don't know what you want in the future. I mean, a few years ago I wanted to be a bloody singer in a band but I don't want to be one now, do I?

WEAVER. Alright, I get your drift and you're right, people do change and so do their attitudes.

GEORGE. I'm right, ain't I?

WEAVER. I just said you was.

Pause.

Can you sing then?

GEORGE. What?

WEAVER. Well you just said you wanted to be a singer; does that mean you can sing then?

GEORGE. Well a bit. I'm not brilliant but I can keep in tune.

WEAVER. Give us a burst then.

GEORGE. What?

WEAVER. Go on, sing me a song.

GEORGE (*laughs*). Leave it out.

WEAVER. Go on.

GEORGE. No.

WEAVER. Why not?

GEORGE. I ain't singing you a song.

WEAVER. Oh go on, don't be shy.

GEORGE. No.

WEAVER. Why not?

GEORGE. I don't want to.

WEAVER. What's the matter, I'm your mate, ain't I?

GEORGE. I know you are but I'm not gonna sing to you; wish I'd never said it now.

WEAVER. Oh go on, George, I'm the only one here, I won't laugh.

GEORGE. I can't just sing a song just like that can I? I mean, I haven't sung in years, and besides, I can't do it without a piano.

WEAVER. What, you play the piano as well?

GEORGE. A bit.

WEAVER. Fuck me! He's full of surprises, ain't he.

GEORGE. It's no big deal.

WEAVER. Alright. If you don't want to sing, I won't force you. I'm not that way inclined, but will you do me a favour, next time we go down The Swan will you give me a little tune?

GEORGE. Have they got a piano in there then?

WEAVER. Course they have; ain't you seen it?

GEORGE. No, we're always in The Crown.

WEAVER. Well they have! So you have to give us a little tune one night.

GEORGE. We'll see.

WEAVER. Just a little bash on the keyboards. No singing. Just a little bash.

GEORGE. I'll see next time we go in there.

WEAVER. That's the spirit. I do love a good sing-song round the piano. You don't find it much these days, it's all that 'rock around the clock' shit, does my fucking head in.

GEORGE. Gordon said he might pop round but he's probably forgotten about it after Derek's party last night.

WEAVER. Bad was he?

GEORGE. Off his head.

WEAVER. I should've been there.

GEORGE. You missed a good piss-up.

WEAVER. Still, nothing I can do about it now.

GEORGE. You'll just have to wait for the next one.

WEAVER. I'll be waiting all year before that tight sod throws another bash.

GEORGE. Well I'd have one but this place is too small.

WEANIER. It's not too small.

GEORGE. It's too small for a party, I can only get about four people in here.

WEAVER. Leave it out. You could fit ten in here if you put your mind to it.

GEORGE. I couldn't have one anyway, my landlady wouldn't like it.

WEAVER. You could have a small gathering though.

GEORGE. Eh?

WEAVER. A small gathering. You know, just a couple of people for a quiet drink and a bite to eat. A sort of dinner party.

GEORGE. I couldn't have a dinner party in here, it's a dump.

WEAVER. Well I don't mean a dinner party exactly, just a couple of people, a few bottles of beer and some titbits. Sounds quite cosy to me.

GEORGE. Yeah but you know what that lot like. I can't just have one or two up here, they'd think I was being out of order.

WEAVER. Well it doesn't have to be that lot, does it?

GEORGE. How do you mean?

WEAVER. Well, it could just be you, me and a couple of birds.

GEORGE. What birds?

WEAVER. I don't know… Janet and her mate.

GEORGE. What mate?

WEAVER. Any mate. You're not fussy are you?

GEORGE. No, I couldn't have any women up here, she wouldn't allow it.

WEAVER. You've had birds up here before ain't you?

GEORGE. I haven't as it goes… See, if I meet a bird I go back to her place, don't I.

WEAVER. Oh, I see. Well I'm sure she wouldn't notice if we slipped them up quietly.

GEORGE. I don't know…

WEAVER. Where's your spirit of adventure? It'd be a laugh.

GEORGE. I'll have to think about it.

WEAVER. I think it's a great idea, can't wait.

GEORGE. I said I'd need to think about it.

WEAVER. That's alright, you have a good think. No need to rush into it, you can't hurry these things can you, they need planning.

Pause.

She loves a good sorting that Janet. Got any more Scotch?

Blackout.

Scene Two

Later that day. WEAVER *is slumped on the bed asleep.*
GEORGE *is sitting in the armchair.* GORDON *enters with two
mugs of tea and shuts the door.*

GORDON. There you are, George, get that down you.

GEORGE. Cheers, Gordon, thanks for bringing the milk.

GORDON. Pleasure. How long has he been here?

GEORGE. Couple of hours. He's been asleep for ages.

GORDON. Don't you mind?

GEORGE. Well I was hoping to clean this place up a bit, but it
can wait.

GORDON. You should wake him up and ask him to leave, he'll
be there all day otherwise.

GEORGE. I'll give him a bit longer. He's had quite a lot to
drink.

GORDON. He can't hold it, he thinks he can but he can't. He
either falls asleep or throws up, sometimes both. I won't
have him in my flat.

GEORGE. Why not?

GORDON. Because once he's in you can never get him out.

GEORGE. He'll go when I ask him.

GORDON. I wouldn't count on it.

GEORGE. He will, I know he will.

GORDON. Oh well, it's your problem.

Pause.

GEORGE. Did you feel rough this morning?

GORDON. Not really, no.

GEORGE. You put away a bit.

GORDON. I'm just lucky I suppose, but then I always remember to drink a pint of water before I go to bed.

GEORGE. Good night wasn't it.

GORDON. Most pleasant. (*Looks at* WEAVER.) And why wasn't he there?

GEORGE. Didn't feel well, couldn't manage it.

GORDON. He must have been bad. I've never known the mighty Weaver to miss a free piss-up before.

GEORGE. He's alright now though.

GORDON. Yes, he looks it.

Pause.

So. Are you coming to see this band with me then?

GEORGE. What band?

GORDON. The one I told you about last night, don't you remember?

GEORGE. I can hardly remember anything about last night.

GORDON. Well, this friend of mine, Pete his name is, I used to drink with him years ago, well he plays the trumpet in a jazz band. I bumped into him the other day and he gave me a couple of free tickets for tonight.

GEORGE. Where is it?

GORDON. A little club that's just opened at the Angel. They're open till two, the drinks are quite cheap, so it should be a good night.

GEORGE. How much is it to get in?

GORDON. I've just told you, I've got two free tickets.

GEORGE. Oh that's handy.

GORDON. Do you want to come then?

GEORGE. Might as well, I've got no other plans.

GORDON. Good, George, good, you won't regret it. He's a wonderful trumpeter and I also thought it was jolly decent of him to give me these tickets, especially as I haven't seen him for so long.

GEORGE. Why ain't you taking Marion?

GORDON. She's gone to her parents for the weekend. Besides, we're always together, it's nice to have a break from each other now and then.

GEORGE. Do you think you'll ever get hitched?

GORDON. I'd like to one day but she's not that keen. She seems to think we're fine as we are. She's right I suppose.

GEORGE. She's a lovely lady, isn't she.

GORDON. Smashing.

GEORGE. Everyone likes her.

GORDON. Well she's so warm and understanding. Never nags, never moans, always there when I need her, and she likes a drink.

GEORGE (*laughs*). Not half.

GORDON. But she never loses control of herself, that's what I like. You know, George, I can't stand some of those women in The Crown who start shouting and screaming after a couple of drinks, either that or they disappear into the ladies' for half an hour.

GEORGE. I've always wondered what they do in there.

GORDON. They cry.

GEORGE. Do they?

GORDON. Oh yes. It's the gin, it sparks off the emotions. They sit there and start pondering on all the awful things that have happened to them, usually it's men, and they start to cry about it. They feel a lot better afterwards, then turn the other way and start laughing at the slightest thing; I find it most infuriating.

GEORGE. I never noticed that before. It's quite funny really. I mean, it's strange how blokes don't act like that.

GORDON. Oh but they do. We're just better at hiding it. Men aren't supposed to show their feelings, it's not the 'done' thing.

Pause.

Have you ever wanted to scream, George?

GEORGE. I don't know what you mean.

GORDON. Have you ever sat in this room, on your own, feeling as though the whole world was against you and just wanted to scream?

GEORGE. I don't know, sort of I suppose.

GORDON. But have you ever done it?

GEORGE. No, no, I haven't.

GORDON. Why not?

GEORGE. I don't know, I'd feel silly.

GORDON. But why feel silly when you're the only one in the room? Nobody's going to hear you, are they? It's such a relief to get it out of your system. I do it all the time.

GEORGE. Well, I'll have to try it the next time I get the hump. (*Changing the subject.*) So, what time are we going to this club then?

GORDON. I could pick you up if you like. We'll get a taxi: the Tube is such a bore. Nine o'clock should be fine.

GEORGE. We could get a bus.

GORDON. Oh no, we'd have to get two and we'd be waiting for ever. A taxi is a much better idea.

GEORGE. Well I haven't got much money, you see.

GORDON. Don't worry, I'll pay.

GEORGE. Oh no I couldn't…

GORDON. I'd be getting a taxi if I went on my own, so it makes very little difference.

GEORGE. If you're sure.

GORDON. Of course I am.

Pause.

You know, I'm rather looking forward to this.

GEORGE. It'll make a nice change, anyway.

Pause.

GORDON. Right. Well, I'll be off then. (*Gets up.*)

GEORGE. Oh, you off then?

GORDON. Better make tracks, yes.

GEORGE. Okay then. (*Gets up.*) I'll see you tonight then.

GORDON. Nine to half past, yes? (*Looks at* WEAVER.) Will you be able to manage him?

GEORGE. Oh yeah, I'll wake him up in a minute and give him a cup of tea. Thanks again for the milk.

GORDON. Think nothing of it.

Pause.

Right. I'll see you later then.

GEORGE. See you later.

Pause.

GORDON. Cheerio. (*Exits.*)

GEORGE. Bye. (*Shuts the door.*)

Pause.

WEAVER. He's such a wanker that bloke.

GEORGE. Oh. You awake?

WEAVER. No.

GEORGE. Have a good kip?

WEAVER. I was sleeping like a baby till he starts going on. He does my head in.

GEORGE. He's alright.

WEAVER. He's an old tosspot. Goes on about fuck-all most of the time.

GEORGE. Do you want a cup of tea?

WEAVER. No, you're alright. (*Sits up. Pause.*) You know he's a queer-boy don't you?

GEORGE. No he isn't.

WEAVER. He is, you know.

GEORGE. He can't be, he goes out with Marion.

WEAVER. Just because he's got a woman doesn't mean he's not into men as well. Come to think of it a lot of 'em have a bird on their arm as a sort of cover-up.

GEORGE. Well I don't believe you.

WEAVER. Fair enough, but don't come running to me when he starts lifting your shirt.

GEORGE. Oh shut up.

Pause.

WEAVER. You going then?

GEORGE. Going where?

WEAVER. This club, with him?

GEORGE. Yeah, sounds like it could be good.

WEAVER. Can I come?

GEORGE. I don't know.

WEAVER. What do you mean by that?

GEORGE. Well he's only got two tickets.

WEAVER. That's alright, I'll pay me own way in and come down with you two in the taxi.

GEORGE. Well it's not up to me, is it.

WEAVER. Gordon won't mind.

GEORGE. How do you know?

WEAVER. He likes me.

GEORGE. Does he?

WEAVER. Yeah, he thinks I'm a laugh, he's always telling me what a laugh I am. He'll be dead chuffed when he knows I'm coming.

GEORGE. Well you can ask him then, 'cos I ain't.

WEAVER. There's no need to ask him is there? I'll just stay here, get cleaned up and wait for him with you.

GEORGE. I don't know, Weaver...

WEAVER. What's the matter with you? He won't mind, I know he won't. Anyway, he can't stop me going can he? He don't own the fucking place. I'll even go there on my own and meet you in there.

GEORGE. Alright.

WEAVER. It's only a poxy jazz club, anyone would think he had tickets to see the Queen fart the way you're going on.

GEORGE. I said alright, Weaver, just forget it.

WEAVER. I just want you to see how silly you're being. Anyway, I would've thought you'd want me to be there. Can't leave you on your own with him, can we?

GEORGE. Oh don't talk soft.

WEAVER. It's because his dick's so small, that's why he's a poof.

GEORGE. What are you going on about?

WEAVER. It's a well-known fact that poofs are the way they are because they've got small dicks. They can't satisfy women you see and I happen to know that Gordon's got the smallest dick in the world.

GEORGE. Well I've seen it and it don't look small to me.

WEAVER. He's got two balls and an helmet.

GEORGE. Oh stop talking crap, Weaver! You do my bloody head in sometimes. Gordon is supposed to be one of your mates so I think it's really unfair that you talk about him like that. Now let's just drop it.

Pause.

WEAVER. Can I borrow a shirt?

GEORGE. Can't you go home and get one?

WEAVER. I only need a fresh shirt, no point in going all the way home just for a fresh shirt is there?

GEORGE. I'll see what I can find.

WEAVER. Clean shirt, quick splash of water on my face and bosh, I'm ready.

There is a knock on the door.

TEBBIT (*off*). George, are you in?

GEORGE. It's my landlady. Sit up properly and fix that bed up.

WEAVER. Alright, alright, don't get jumpy.

GEORGE (*shouts*). Is that you, Mrs Tebbit?

TEBBIT (*off*). Yes. Can I come in?

GEORGE. Hold on a mo. (*Opens the door and lets her in.*)

TEBBIT. Oh sorry to disturb you, George. I didn't know you still had company. Afternoon, Mr Weaver.

WEAVER. Afternoon, Mrs Tebbit. Rotten day, ain't it?

TEBBIT. Lovely for ducks though.

WEAVER. Yeah, it would be if it was raining.

GEORGE. What can I do for you then?

TEBBIT. This letter came for you.

GEORGE. Oh, thank you.

TEBBIT. It's postmarked Brighton, so it must be from your sister.

GEORGE. Yes it is, I can tell by the writing.

TEBBIT. Nice getting letters, isn't it?

GEORGE. Lovely.

TEBBIT. I like getting letters. Much nicer than talking on the phone. I'm not very good at writing them though.

GEORGE. No, me neither.

WEAVER. I'm quite a good letter-writer myself.

TEBBIT. That's probably why I don't get many.

WEAVER. Oh that's a shame.

TEBBIT. Still, it's my own fault, shouldn't moan. Anyway, I just thought I'd better bring it up to you.

GEORGE. Well that's very kind of you, thank you very much.

TEBBIT. It's my pleasure, George. Well. I'd better get back to my business, I've got this cabbage on the boil. Sorry to disturb you.

GEORGE. That's alright, you pop up any time you feel the need.

TEBBIT. I'll see you later then.

WEAVER. Take care.

TEBBIT. I'll try. (*Exits.*)

WEAVER. Not a bad old sort is it?

GEORGE (*sits and opens the letter*). Yeah, she's alright.

    Pause.

WEAVER. Can I have a bath?

GEORGE. What?

WEAVER. Would it be alright if I had a bath?

GEORGE. Not really, no.

WEAVER. Oh. Alright then.

GEORGE. It's not up to me you see. if it was my bath I'd say yes, but we have to share it you see...

WEAVER. That's alright, I understand.

GEORGE. Sorry.

WEAVER. Don't worry about it. Read your letter. (*He gets up and wanders around the room. Goes to the wardrobe, opens it, rummages inside, then holds out a shirt.*) Can I wear this?

GEORGE. What?

WEAVER. This shirt, can I wear it tonight?

GEORGE. If you like.

WEAVER. You sure you don't want to wear it?

GEORGE. I'm wearing the blue one.

WEAVER. What blue one?

GEORGE. That one there, near your left hand.

WEAVER (*takes out the shirt*). Oh yeah, that's nice ain't it. So you don't mind if I have this one then?

GEORGE. Course not.

WEAVER. Cheers, that'll go nice with me slacks.

There is a knock on the door.

TEBBIT (*off*). George?

GEORGE (*to* WEAVER). Open the door.

WEAVER. Yes, Mrs Tebbit.

TEBBIT. Oh thank you, Mr Weaver. I'm ever so sorry to disturb you again, George.

GEORGE. That's alright. What can I do for you?

TEBBIT. I knew there was something I wanted to ask you but it went right out of my head before. You must think I'm a bit of a pain.

GEORGE. Don't be silly. Would you care to sit down?

TEBBIT. No thank you, it won't take a minute. (*She sits in the chair*.) The thing is, I'm a bit worried about Mr Thomas.

GEORGE. Mr Thomas?

TEBBIT. Yes, you know, the gentleman who lives in the room below you.

GEORGE. Oh I know, yes?

TEBBIT. Well the thing is, I haven't seen him since last night and he's not in his room because I've knocked.

GEORGE. Have you looked inside?

TEBBIT. Well yes I have. I know I shouldn't but I was worried you see. Anyway, he's not there.

WEAVER. Perhaps he's done a bunk.

TEBBIT. Oh no, he wouldn't do that. His rent's all paid up. He likes to pay monthly because that's how his work pays him and he's still got two weeks of this month left.

GEORGE. Perhaps he's gone on a little holiday.

TEBBIT. That's what I thought at first, but all his clothes are still there. The only thing that's missing is the suit he wears for work. I do his washing for him you see, just as a sideline, he gives me a couple of bob for it.

WEAVER. Oh that's handy.

TEBBIT. I was hoping that you might have seen him, George.

GEORGE. I don't see him that much anyway.

TEBBIT. Yes. He's a very private person.

GEORGE. I never see him use the cooker either.

TEBBIT. That's because he likes to eat out. He always has his dinner in a restaurant.

WEAVER. Well it's alright for some, ain't it?

GEORGE. I can't help you, I'm afraid.

TEBBIT. I know this may sound dramatic but do you think I should inform the police?

WEAVER. What for?

TEBBIT. To tell them he's gone missing.

WEAVER. Well he's not been gone long and he is a grown man. You never know, he might have pulled a bird and stayed with her for the night.

TEBBIT. I couldn't see him doing that, he's not the type. He's very religious you see, he reads the Bible before he has his hot milk.

WEAVER. Even religious men get the urge.

GEORGE. He could be right, you know.

TEBBIT. I don't think so...

WEAVER. He's a human, ain't he?

TEBBIT. But he's not the type!

WEAVER. Let me tell you something, darling. No matter how a man may appear on the outside we're all the same on the inside. We all have the same thoughts and we're all after the same thing. I'm right ain't I, George?

GEORGE. Well...

WEAVER. I bet that's where he is. Don't worry about it.

TEBBIT. I know I shouldn't but I can't help it. He's such a nice man, I'd hate to think something had happened to him.

WEAVER. Nothing's happened to him. You care too much about others, that's your problem.

TEBBIT. I do yes, it's in my water.

GEORGE. Look. Give it another couple of days and if he doesn't show up by then, call the police.

TEBBIT. I suppose I am being a little hasty.

WEAVER. Of course you are. I'll tell you one thing though, I wish I had a lovely lady like you worrying about me.

TEBBIT. Oh, Mr Weaver, you are kind.

WEAVER. It's the truth.

TEBBIT. You do say the nicest things, doesn't he say the nicest things, George?

GEORGE. He does that. He's a right charmer.

WEAVER. I've just got respect for people that's all.

TEBBIT (*gets up*). Well thanks, anyway. Sorry to bother you again.

WEAVER. It's no bother, stop being a silly billy. As George said, you come up any time, it's your house, ain't it.

TEBBIT. You are kind.

WEAVER. Not at all.

TEBBIT. If Mr Thomas doesn't come back you're quite welcome to have his room, it's very cheap.

WEAVER. That's very nice of you, I'll keep it in mind.

TEBBIT. Cheerio then. (*Exits.*)

WEAVER. What a lovely lady. Attractive too… if you look properly.

Blackout.

Scene Three

That evening. WEAVER *is combing his hair in front of the mirror.* GORDON *is in the armchair.*

WEAVER. We wasn't expecting you till nine see, that's why we ain't ready yet.

GORDON. That's alright, my fault.

WEAVER. So you don't mind me coming then?

GORDON. Not at all. I've only got the two tickets though.

WEAVER. That's okay. I'll pay my own way in.

GORDON. Fine.

WEAVER. And Brenda.

GORDON. I'm sorry?

WEAVER. I'll pay for Brenda as well.

GORDON. Who is Brenda?

WEAVER. Oh sorry… I didn't tell you did I? I've asked George's landlady along as well. I hope you don't mind.

GORDON. Well, no…

WEAVER. She's a bit down you see. Got a few problems with one of the tenants. I thought a night out might cheer her up. She was quite chuffed when I asked her.

GORDON. I'm sure she was.

WEAVER. Ever met her?

GORDON. A couple of times.

WEAVER. She's a lovely woman, you know. There's a really nice gentleness about her, do you know what I mean? She seems quite lonely though you'd never think it, puts on a brave face and all that. Between you and me Gordon, I could see myself getting quite fond of her. She's my kind of woman you see, I sussed that this afternoon. I'd never really noticed it before but she's quite sexy. I think she's got it in her to be a right little raver.

GORDON. How interesting.

WEAVER. Funny how you spot these things ain't it? Still, she could do with a night out.

GORDON. It was most thoughtful of you to ask her.

WEAVER. Yeah, I'm good like that.

Pause.

Do you like this shirt?

GORDON. Oh yes, it's very nice.

WEAVER. George lent it to me. Do you think the colour suits me?

GORDON. Very becoming.

WEAVER. I've never seen him wear it though, have you? He probably don't like it. I might as well ask him if I can keep it, do you think he'd mind?

GORDON. No harm in trying, I suppose.

WEAVER. I'll ask him later. No point in him keeping it if he don't wear it is there?

Pause.

I like your shoes.

GORDON. Do you?

WEAVER. Lovely.

GORDON. Thank you.

WEAVER. New, are they?

GORDON. I bought them yesterday.

WEAVER. Expensive?

GORDON. Not very.

WEAVER. The stitching looks good, important that.

GORDON. Very.

WEAVER. Did you get them from Brownings?

GORDON. As a matter of fact I did.

WEAVER. Thought so; that's a good shop. Yep, that's a very good pair of shoes you've got there.

GORDON. Thank you.

GEORGE *enters, looking very smart.*

WEAVER. Here he is. Oh don't he look dapper!

GEORGE. Sorry I took so long.

GORDON. Not to worry, I'm early.

WEAVER. Have you seen Gordon's new shoes?

GEORGE. Yeah I saw them last night. Blimey, they've got a bit scuffed haven't they?

GORDON. I went for a walk during the party and fell in a bloody ditch.

WEAVER (*laughs under breath*). Silly cunt.

GORDON. What time is it?

GEORGE. About quarter-past eight.

GORDON. Gosh, I am early.

GEORGE. We can have a drink here before we go.

WEAVER. Good idea. Shall I go downstairs and see if Brenda's ready?

GEORGE. Might as well. See if she wants a drink too.

WEAVER. I'll do that then. Do I look alright?

GEORGE. You look fine.

WEAVER. Right then. Back in a minute. (*Exits.*)

GORDON. Well. This is a right bugger-up.

GEORGE. What is?

GORDON. Oh come on, George, you know very well what I mean. Why did you ask Weaver to come?

GEORGE. I didn't ask him. He sort of invited himself.

GORDON. How did he find out about it then?

GEORGE. He heard us talking. He was awake.

GORDON. The sneaky little bastard.

GEORGE. It doesn't matter does it?

GORDON. Of course it matters! This is a respectable club with respectable people. You know what he's like when he's had a few drinks; there's no telling what he might get up to.

GEORGE. He'll be alright. He'll have Mrs Tebbit with him so he'll be on his best behaviour, I know he will. He wants to impress her, doesn't he.

GORDON. I still think he's got a nerve.

GEORGE. It was a bit cheeky, but there was nothing I could do about it.

GORDON. I know. I'm not blaming you, George, but I do think you should be a little harder with him; don't let him get his own way so much.

GEORGE. Sorry.

GORDON. Well there's nothing we can do about it now.

Pause.

God, I hate that man.

GEORGE. Do you? He thinks you like him.

GORDON. Well he would, wouldn't he. He's a nasty piece of work, George, believe me.

GEORGE. He's not that bad, you've just never seen the nice side of him.

GORDON. I don't believe he has one.

GEORGE. You should give him a chance, you know.

GORDON. Why do you always stand up for him?

GEORGE. Well he's my mate, isn't he. He's never done me any harm.

GORDON. Give it time.

GEORGE. Look. I'm sorry you've got the hump about him coming, but, like I said, there was nothing I could do about it. Anyway, it might be quite a laugh with him and Mrs Tebbit. I couldn't believe it when he asked her along. She looked right chuffed about it as well.

GORDON. So I believe.

GEORGE. It was good of him though and she's not a bad sort. She's a bit worried about one of the blokes that lives here.

GORDON. Yes, the weasel did mention it.

GEORGE. A night out will take her mind off things.

Pause.

GORDON. May I have that drink now please?

GEORGE. Oh yeah, sorry. Vodka alright?

GORDON. Fine.

GEORGE (*gets the drink, mugs, etc.*). Do you want tonic in it?

GORDON. Please.

GEORGE. There you go.

GORDON. Oh, thank you.

Pause.

Look. I'm sorry for being such an old stick-in-the-mud, but you do understand don't you?

GEORGE. Course. Let's just forget about it and have a good time.

GORDON. You're right, as always. It's the best thing to do.

WEAVER (*enters*). She'll be up in a minute, just getting her bag.

GEORGE. Do you want a drink?

WEAVER. Wouldn't mind. She don't half look tasty.

GEORGE. Yeah?

WEAVER. A right little cracker. I was quite surprised. I knew she had it in her though. You'd better pour her out one of them; she'll be here in a minute.

GEORGE. Righty-oh. (*Hands* WEAVER *a drink*.)

WEAVER. Cheers, Georgy-boy. I need this. I know it sounds soppy but I think I'm a little bit nervous. I want to impress her I suppose.

GORDON. You'll have to be on your best behaviour then.

WEAVER. Oh yeah. I'm gonna take it easy with the old booze alright.

GORDON. Good idea.

WEAVER. Besides, I might get a result later and I don't want anything letting me down do I? (*Laughs crudely*.)

There is a knock on the door. GEORGE *opens it.* TEBBIT *walks in looking very different from the first time we saw her. She looks stunning.*

TEBBIT. Evening, George.

GEORGE. Blimey, you look nice.

TEBBIT. Thank you.

WEAVER. What did I tell you, bit of alright ain't she?

TEBBIT (*loving it*). Mr Weaver!

WEAVER. You sit down in that chair you little sexpot.

TEBBIT (*sits*). Oh isn't he terrible, George.

GEORGE (*hands her a drink in an old tin mug*). It's a vodka and tonic, I hope you like it. Now, you've met Mr Davis before haven't you.

TEBBIT. A couple of times, yes.

GORDON (*shakes her hand*). Pleased to meet you again.

TEBBIT. And you, Mr Davis.

GORDON. Please, call me Gordon.

TEBBIT. And I'm Brenda.

Pause.

GORDON. I hope you don't mind my saying, and I'm sure we're all agreed, but that really is the most lovely dress.

TEBBIT. Oh thank you, Gordon. I've had it for quite a few years now but luckily I've managed to retain my figure. I don't get the chance to wear it that often. Tonight is quite a treat.

GORDON. I was most delighted to hear that you and Weaver were to be joining us. It should be a lovely evening.

TEBBIT. You know someone in the band, I believe.

GORDON. Yes, the trumpet player.

TEBBIT. Is he good?

GORDON. First class. He's a very old friend.

TEBBIT. Will we get to meet him?

GORDON. Of course. He'll have a drink with us when he's finished his spot.

TEBBIT. Oh how exciting! I've never met a proper musician before.

WEAVER. I've got a mate who plays the drums.

GEORGE. Have you? You never told me.

WEAVER. Well I don't like to brag about it do I! He's over in America at the moment making quite a name for himself. I'll have to introduce you to him, Brenda, if he comes back for a holiday or something.

TEBBIT. Oh. That would be lovely.

Pause.

GORDON. Have you lived here long, Brenda?

TEBBIT. All my life. The house belonged to my parents; they took in boarders as well. When they passed on I decided to keep it going. I'm not trained to do anything else anyway.

GORDON. And what about your husband?

TEBBIT. Husband?

GORDON. Well you are Mrs Tebbit not Miss.

TEBBIT. Oh I see. No, I just call myself Mrs to gain respect. I was engaged once but he was killed in action during the war.

GORDON. Oh I am sorry.

WEAVER. So am I.

TEBBIT. At least here I'm always surrounded by people, I'm never alone.

WEAVER. Well that's one good thing, there's nothing worse than being on your tod.

TEBBIT. I do regret not marrying and having children. I would've liked to have someone to pass the house on to, if you see what I mean.

WEAVER. There's still plenty of time for that, I mean you're not old or anything are you?

TEBBIT. You are kind, Mr Weaver, but I'm quite a bit older than I look.

WEAVER. How old are you then?

TEBBIT. That's not the sort of question you should ask a lady.

WEAVER. Whoops, beg your pardon.

TEBBIT. Well, not on the first date anyway.

WEAVER. Can I ask you something else then? Would you ever let one of your tenants have a party?

TEBBIT. How do you mean?

WEAVER. Well not a party party but a little drink-up sort of thing, a little gathering.

TEBBIT. Well George is having one now and I'm one of the guests, so I'd be wrong to object.

WEAVER. There you are, George, I told you. He didn't think you'd allow it.

TEBBIT. Well I'd need to be told about it in advance. Are you thinking of having one then?

GEORGE. No. We were just talking about it, that's all.

WEAVER. He worries too much you see, cares too much about other people.

TEBBIT. Well I would say that's a good quality to have.

WEAVER. Oh so would I. He's a good bloke is George, I'm always telling him that.

TEBBIT. He's lovely.

WEAVER. Smashing.

GORDON. Oh look, you're embarrassing him.

GEORGE. Oh I don't mind, it's quite nice really.

WEAVER. That's the spirit, Georgy-boy.

Pause.

Right then. I think we should hit the road.

GORDON. Good idea.

TEBBIT. How are we getting there?

WEAVER. Taxi.

TEBBIT. Oh how grand.

WEAVER. Only the best for you, my lovely.

GORDON. I shall be paying for it though.

WEAVER. Right and all, you're the one with the free tickets, I've got to pay for me and her to get into the gaff.

There is a knock on the door.

GORDON. Did somebody knock?

GEORGE. I think so.

TEBBIT. Are you expecting anyone else?

GEORGE. No.

Another knock.

WEAVER. Well you'd better see who it is then, mate.

GEORGE. Yeah. Sorry.

GEORGE *opens the door. A man covered in dirt and dried blood stands in the doorway for a few seconds before falling on the floor into the room.*

TEBBIT. Fuck me! It's Mr Thomas!

Blackout.

Interval.

ACT TWO

Scene One

Later that night. GEORGE *is in the armchair drinking vodka.*
After a few moments TEBBIT *enters.*

GEORGE. How is he?

TEBBIT. Not too bad. He's gone to sleep.

GEORGE. Has he told you anything?

TEBBIT. Not yet. It's terrible not knowing.

GEORGE. We should call the police.

TEBBIT. That's what I keep telling him but he doesn't want me
to. I can hardly go against his wishes can I?

GEORGE. I suppose not.

TEBBIT. Anyway, he might feel differently in the morning; he
might want me to fetch them then. He's a very proud man
you see, he likes to keep himself clean and tidy. He was very
embarrassed about us all seeing him in that state.

GEORGE. That's silly, it's not his fault, is it.

TEBBIT. I know but some men are funny like that.

Pause.

He'd messed his trousers.

GEORGE. Oh dear.

TEBBIT. Poor thing. He didn't know where to look.

GEORGE. Did you clean him up then?

TEBBIT. Yes.

GEORGE. That was good of you.

TEBBIT. I didn't mind. I couldn't really leave him like he was, could I?

GEORGE. No, I suppose not. It was still good of you, though.

TEBBIT. I don't mind doing my bit.

GEORGE. Would you like a drink?

TEBBIT. I don't think I should, I've had a couple already.

GEORGE. Go on, you deserve one.

TEBBIT. I'm not used to it, you see.

GEORGE. I insist, it'll calm you down.

TEBBIT. I suppose I am a bit shaky. Go on then, just a small one, mind.

GEORGE. That's the spirit. (*Gets up and pours a drink.*)

TEBBIT. I'm sorry you missed seeing the band.

GEORGE. Well you missed it too.

TEBBIT. It's not the same thing though, is it.

GEORGE. I couldn't leave you alone with Mr Thomas. It was my duty to stay with you, what with being one of your tenants and that.

TEBBIT. At least the tickets won't go to waste. I do like your friends but I'm glad they're out of the way.

GEORGE. Not much help were they?

TEBBIT. Well some men are like that, George, the sight of blood makes them go funny. I'm lucky to have such a strong tummy; yours must be quite strong too.

GEORGE (*starts to giggle*). Oh dear.

TEBBIT. What?

GEORGE. Nothing.

TEBBIT. What you laughing at?

GEORGE. I was just wondering how Gordon and Weaver are getting on.

TEBBIT. How do you mean?

GEORGE. They can't stand each other.

TEBBIT. Really?

GEORGE. Yeah, they hate each other. They've never got on, they pretend they do, but they don't.

TEBBIT. How funny, I thought they were really good friends.

GEORGE. Well now you know.

TEBBIT. They both like you though, don't they?

GEORGE. I think so.

TEBBIT. Oh they do. Gordon thinks the world of you.

GEORGE. I don't know why, I'm nothing special.

TEBBIT. Well that's just it, you're not a threat.

GEORGE. What do you mean?

TEBBIT. Well, you're not flashy like Weaver and you're not a ladies' man like Gordon.

GEORGE. I don't know how to take that.

TEBBIT. Take it as a compliment, it's meant as one. You're a lovely man, George, the sooner you realise that the better.

GEORGE. I think I'm boring.

TEBBIT. You're not boring.

GEORGE. I bore myself sometimes. I've never done anything with my life, don't suppose I ever will.

TEBBIT. You've got friends, haven't you?

GEORGE. A few, yes.

TEBBIT. Well that's an achievement in itself. It's not easy making friends you know. I haven't got any.

GEORGE. I don't believe that, you must have.

TEBBIT. Don't get me wrong, I've got acquaintances, I've got lots of them but I haven't got what you'd call a real friend, you know, someone who comes round for a cup of tea and a natter. I used to have one. Her name was Betty. We were mates at school together and all that. We had a bit of a tiff about twelve years ago. She got married, moved to Wales and I haven't seen or heard from her since.

GEORGE. That's a shame. What did you row about?

TEBBIT. A fella. He was one of the tenants. He'd only been here a couple of months and he took a fancy to me, if you see what I mean. Well, I wasn't interested at first because my fiancé had only been laid to rest for a short while so it would've looked bad if I'd started walking out with other men so soon after.

GEORGE. Yes, it would a bit.

TEBBIT. Anyway, I told Betty that I liked him but wanted to leave it for a while before I started seeing him. She told him I didn't like him at all so he started taking her out instead. I thought it was terrible of her to do such a thing so I stopped talking to her. I know it's silly now, but when you're young you take these things so seriously don't you. There hasn't been anyone else since then. I went out with the man who reads the meter a couple of times, but we wasn't well matched. Weaver is the first man I've had a date with in five years.

GEORGE. Blimey.

TEBBIT. I don't mean to sound big-headed or anything but I know that quite a few of the men who have stayed here have had their eye on me but they never do anything about it. I'm sure they think I'm some kind of old bag because I'm a landlady.

GEORGE. It could be that they don't think you're interested in them. You are a very attractive lady, if you don't mind me saying so.

TEBBIT. That's a lovely thing to say. I've been quite spoilt tonight with all the flattery that's been chucked about. I won't be able to get my head out of the door.

GEORGE. It hasn't been much of a date for you has it?

TEBBIT. I don't mind. I'm glad I was here when Mr Thomas came back. Anyway, I'm quite enjoying myself, having this little drink with you.

GEORGE. So am I. I don't know why we haven't done it before.

TEBBIT. We should do it again.

GEORGE. Oh yes, we should.

TEBBIT. Or you could come down to my flat one night and I could cook you a meal, I haven't used my roasting pan in years.

GEORGE. That would be lovely.

TEBBIT. You could bring your lady friend as well, that's if you've got one.

GEORGE. No, no I haven't.

TEBBIT. I thought not. You're too young to tie yourself down. Enjoy yourself while you're young. I wish I had.

GEORGE. I would like to have someone, you know, a sort of steady, but I'm not much good with girls.

TEBBIT. I don't believe that, you're alright with me, ain't you?

GEORGE. Yeah but that's different, I know you.

TEBBIT. Not that well.

GEORGE. But I know who you are, sort of thing. See, I don't think most women take me seriously, I'm just someone to confide in, I'm a good listener you see. I was really hooked on this woman Marion for a while. We used to have really good chats. I think I sort of fell in love with her, but she goes out with Gordon. I used to hate listening to him talking about her, but I'm alright about it now. Got over it I suppose.

TEBBIT. Did she know how you felt about her?

GEORGE. I don't think so. I never told her anyway, never told anyone, not even Weaver, and I tell him most things.

TEBBIT. I'm flattered.

GEORGE. What for?

TEBBIT. Well you just told me a secret, that means you trust me. Oh I've come over all warm.

GEORGE. Oh. That's nice.

Pause.

TEBBIT. Can I have a look through your collection?

GEORGE. I beg your pardon?

TEBBIT. Your records. Can I see what you've got?

GEORGE. Oh of course. They're a bit old I'm afraid, can't remember the last time I bought one.

TEBBIT. Blimey, they are old ain't they. (*Holds up a record.*) Oh I really like this one. Can I put it on?

GEORGE. What is it? Oh yeah, I like that one. It is a bit old isn't it, must be one of Weaver's. Here, I'll put it on for you.

TEBBIT *sits down and* GEORGE *starts cleaning the record, etc.*

GEORGE. Here, I'll tell you what. Why don't we have a little dance?

TEBBIT. For someone who isn't good with girls, you're doing alright.

GEORGE. Yeah but you're…

TEBBIT. I know, I'm different. Oh why not. We would've had one at the club wouldn't we?

GEORGE. I don't know about that, Weaver probably wouldn't let anyone else go near you.

TEBBIT. Well he isn't here now so we might as well. I might not be very good mind, I haven't danced with anyone in years.

GEORGE. That's alright. Neither have I.

The record starts to play: 'It Only Happens When I Dance With You' by Irving Berlin. They both stand self-consciously, then put their arms around each other. They move well together. TEBBIT *starts to run her fingers through* GEORGE's *hair. He looks scared but is also enjoying it. After a few seconds* THOMAS *enters in his pyjamas with a make-shift bandage on his head.* GEORGE *quickly switches off the record player.*

THOMAS. Oh I'm so sorry, I didn't mean to disturb you, I was just wondering if I might have a cup of tea?

Blackout.

Scene Two

THOMAS *is in the armchair and* GEORGE *is on the end of the bed. An embarrassed silence. After a few moments* TEBBIT *enters with a cup of tea.*

TEBBIT. There you are, Mr Thomas, that should make you feel better.

THOMAS. Thank you, Brenda, you are kind.

TEBBIT. I thought you was asleep.

THOMAS. I couldn't. Too many thoughts swimming around in my head.

TEBBIT. Oh. I see.

Pause.

GEORGE. What happened?

THOMAS. I'd really rather not talk about it. I hope you don't think I'm being rude.

GEORGE. Course not. You just sit there and drink your tea.

THOMAS. Thank you.

TEBBIT. I must say I was quite worried about you, Mr Thomas. if you wasn't back here by tomorrow I would've had the police in.

THOMAS. Oh please you mustn't do that, I really don't want to get them involved.

TEBBIT. Why ever not?

THOMAS. I just don't, that's all.

TEBBIT. Well, it's up to you I suppose. I'm not going to force you into anything you don't want to do.

THOMAS. Who were those two gentlemen who were here earlier?

TEBBIT. They're friends of George, we were all on our way out when you dropped in.

THOMAS. Where are they now?

GEORGE. Gone on to a club. They had a couple of free tickets you see, seemed a pity to waste them.

THOMAS. But you helped me downstairs didn't you?

GEORGE. Yes, me and Gordon.

TEBBIT. And I cleaned you up.

THOMAS. Yes, I remember that. Thank you.

TEBBIT. My pleasure.

THOMAS. I'm so sorry. I've ruined your evening.

TEBBIT. Oh don't be silly. I'm just glad you're back here safe and sound. This place wouldn't be the same without you, would it, George?

GEORGE. Well I don't know really…

TEBBIT. You're always so polite and you keep up with your rent payments. I don't know what I'd do without you, really I don't.

THOMAS *starts to cry.*

TEBBIT. Mr Thomas! Whatever is the matter?

THOMAS. I'm sorry, I'm so sorry.

TEBBIT (*goes over and puts her arm around him*). There, there. It can't be that bad. What are you crying for?

THOMAS. I don't know, I just feel like letting it all out, I'm so sorry.

TEBBIT. Don't keep saying sorry all the time, you're not doing anyone any harm are you?

THOMAS. I just feel such a fool that's all.

TEBBIT. Well don't. If you feel like having a little cry you do that. We don't mind, do we, George?

GEORGE. Course not. You carry on.

TEBBIT. See. No point in bottling it all up is there? (*She rocks him.*) You let it all out. Don't mind us, it'll do you good.

GEORGE. Would you like a drop of vodka?

THOMAS. No, no thank you.

TEBBIT. What about brandy? That might help.

GEORGE. I ain't got any brandy.

TEBBIT. You could pop down the off-licence and get some, I'll pay. Would you like some, Cyril, it'd do you good?

THOMAS. I don't want you to go to any trouble.

TEBBIT. George doesn't mind, do you, George?

GEORGE. Course not. it's only down the road, won't take me a minute.

THOMAS. Well it would be nice, I suppose.

TEBBIT. There, that's what I wanted to hear. (*Gets her bag.*) Here's some money, George, just get a normal bottle, nothing fancy.

GEORGE. Righty-oh.

TEBBIT. And here's the key to my flat. On your way back pop in and get a glass out of the cabinet in my front room. Can't ask him to drink out of a mug, being in that state.

GEORGE. Right. I'll be back in a minute then. (*Whispering.*) Will you be alright with him?

TEBBIT. Course I will. Don't take too long, though.

GEORGE. See you in a minute then. (*Exits.*)

TEBBIT. He's a good boy, isn't he.

THOMAS. Yes.

TEBBIT. You'll feel better with a drop of brandy in you. It always helps in times like these. (*She wanders around the room, goes to the wardrobe and starts to rummage through*

GEORGE*'s belongings*.) Do you want to tell your Auntie Brenda what happened?

THOMAS. Not really.

TEBBIT. It might help.

THOMAS. I doubt it.

TEBBIT. Come on, Cyril. I'm your friend, ain't I?

THOMAS. Of course you are.

TEBBIT. And you trust me, don't you?

THOMAS. Of course I do.

TEBBIT. I wouldn't tell anyone.

THOMAS. I know you wouldn't.

TEBBIT. And we've always got on.

THOMAS. Always.

TEBBIT. So tell me what happened.

THOMAS. I don't want to.

TEBBIT. Why not?

THOMAS. I just don't.

TEBBIT. That's a feeble excuse.

THOMAS. It's not meant to be an excuse.

TEBBIT. So tell me.

THOMAS. I can't.

TEBBIT. You mean you won't.

THOMAS. No, I want to but I can't. You wouldn't like it.

TEBBIT. Why wouldn't I?

THOMAS. Because it's not very pleasant.

TEBBIT. I can take it.

THOMAS. I don't think so.

TEBBIT. Try me.

THOMAS. Please! I can't talk about it yet. It's too soon.

TEBBIT (*sits on the bed*). Funny, I've never thought of you as being weak.

THOMAS. What do you mean?

TEBBIT. I always thought you were strong, could face up to things. Seems I got the wrong impression.

THOMAS. I am strong, Brenda, very strong, it's just…

TEBBIT. What?

THOMAS. I'm scared you won't like me any more.

TEBBIT. Now why ever should I feel like that?

THOMAS (*crying*). Oh, Brenda! I feel so humiliated, so confused. I feel as though I don't want to go on any more!

TEBBIT. Now come on. That's enough of that. I won't have that sort of talk, not in my house, it's not proper. Look. What happened? Did you attack someone? Take advantage of a lady in distress?

THOMAS. Of course not. I'd never hurt anyone. Surely you know that?

TEBBIT. Well of course I do, love, but I mean, what am I to think? I didn't mean to offend you.

THOMAS. I know, I know.

TEBBIT. So what happened then?

Pause.

THOMAS. You see, it was my own fault. I provoked the attack… I was the one who has hurt, but it was my own fault. That's why I can't go to the police.

TEBBIT. But surely if you was the victim…

THOMAS. No, it's the circumstances. Under the circumstances I can't do anything about it. It was probably God punishing me.

TEBBIT. I hate to say this, Cyril, but I think I'm a bit more confused than you are.

THOMAS. Oh this is all wrong! I should never have told you.

TEBBIT. But you haven't told me anything. I don't know what the hell you're going on about. I wish you'd make yourself clearer, Cyril, this is bloody frustrating for me you know!

THOMAS. Please, don't shout.

TEBBIT. Sorry. I lost control of myself then. Don't know what came over me, I'm usually so patient.

THOMAS. I know you are. You should know the truth, you've been so kind to me and I know I can trust you.

TEBBIT. Please, you just take your time. I'm only here to listen. I'll understand.

THOMAS. You see, Brenda, I'm not like other men...

TEBBIT. I know. You're lovely, I wish there was more like you.

THOMAS. That's very kind of you but that's not what I mean. You see... I 'go' with other men... I 'go' with them and last night I 'went' with one and he beat me up.

TEBBIT. Oh dear.

THOMAS. I... I'm 'that' way you see and I've always been 'that' way and I do 'it' with other men.

TEBBIT. Oh dear.

THOMAS. I know you must be shocked, I know you probably think I'm dirty or something, but I can't help the way I am.

TEBBIT. Oh dear, oh dear.

THOMAS. If you want me to move out I'll do it. I mean, I would understand if you didn't want me to live here any more.

Pause.

I'm not ashamed of myself, of being the way I am, I used to be but I'm not any more. I'm just ashamed of you seeing me in this state, this is more unbearable than being beaten up. I've always looked up to you, Brenda, but if you want me to go I will... Now, please be honest with me, for your sake as well as mine.

TEBBIT. Of course I don't want you to go. I am shocked, I'll admit that, I'd be a liar if I said otherwise, but I don't want you to go.

Pause.

Oh you poor man. You poor, poor man. What you must have been through.

THOMAS. I've been to hell and back.

TEBBIT. Oh I can imagine.

THOMAS. You do understand don't you?

TEBBIT. Well, as much as I possibly can.

THOMAS. I knew you would, I should never have doubted you.

TEBBIT. Well, I don't blame you for being apprehensive. There are some who wouldn't have taken it so well.

THOMAS. You've hit the nail on the head there.

TEBBIT. But what I don't understand is why? Why did that man beat you up?

THOMAS. Well at first I thought he was yet another queer-basher.

TEBBIT. I beg your pardon?

THOMAS. A queer-basher. They wait to be picked up by men like me and then they beat us up because of the way we are.

TEBBIT. Really? I don't believe you.

THOMAS. Oh it's quite true, I can assure you.

TEBBIT. But that's terrible.

THOMAS. I know, but it happens all the time.

TEBBIT. Well you learn something new every day. I don't get out much you see.

THOMAS. Anyway he wasn't one of them. You see, I recognised him, I thought I knew him from somewhere and I told him. That was a mistake, I can see that now. See with him, it's not only the police finding out. He wouldn't want anyone to find out because he'd be frightened, you know, frightened that they would think he wasn't a 'real' man.

TEBBIT. I see.

THOMAS. That man obviously thought I'd tell someone so he tried to kill me.

TEBBIT. Kill you?!

THOMAS. Oh he definitely tried to kill me. He hit me over the head with a brick.

TEBBIT. Oh dear.

THOMAS. I wouldn't have told anyone, I'm not the sort, but he must have thought otherwise.

TEBBIT. But you must go to the police, he might do it to someone else.

THOMAS. No I won't do that, I can't do that. I'm perfectly alright, he didn't hit me as hard as he thought. The cut's not that deep, I won't even need a stitch in it. My ribs hurt where he kicked me, but I don't think anything's broken. I'm just bruised a little, that's all.

TEBBIT. Oh, Mr Thomas, you are brave, I must say.

THOMAS. He won't do it again, I know he won't. He was just *scared* that's all, *scared out of his mind*.

TEBBIT. Where did you know him from?

THOMAS. Oh just around. You know, around and about.

TEBBIT. Do you know him well?

THOMAS. No, I'd just seen him around, I knew his face.

TEBBIT. I see.

Pause.

THOMAS. Thank you, Brenda.

TEBBIT. What for?

THOMAS. For everything.

TEBBIT. Go away you old soft-pot. It was my pleasure.

THOMAS. You know, you really are quite wonderful, I feel I...

GEORGE (*enters and is rather out of breath*). There, didn't take long did I?

TEBBIT. You must have ran all the way.

GEORGE. I did. You feeling any better?

THOMAS. Much better thank you, George.

GEORGE. Glad to hear it. I got the brandy.

TEBBIT. Good boy. (*She pours some out for* THOMAS.) There you are, Cyril, that should make you feel better.

THOMAS. Thank you. Are you going to join me?

TEBBIT. Might as well. Do you want some, George?

GEORGE. Wouldn't say no. That's if you don't mind.

TEBBIT. Of course I don't, silly bugger.

GEORGE. Right then. (*Goes through the process of pouring the drinks, then hands one to* TEBBIT.)

TEBBIT (*after a long embarrassed silence*). Well this is cosy isn't it?

THOMAS. Very. I feel much better now, more relaxed.

TEBBIT. Good. It helps to talk.

GEORGE. Had a chat about it, did you?

TEBBIT. Yes, Mr Thomas got it off his chest.

GEORGE. Are you going to the police then?

TEBBIT. No. Mr Thomas and I decided it would be best to leave it.

THOMAS. I just want to try and forget about it, George.

GEORGE. Oh.

TEBBIT. He just needs to clear the whole thing from his mind.

GEORGE. Oh well. You know best.

TEBBIT. I've just had a thought, George. I think it would be a good idea if Cyril slept up here tonight so that you could keep an eye on him.

THOMAS. Oh no, Brenda, there's really no need…

GEORGE. I don't mind.

THOMAS. No really, I don't think it's necessary…

TEBBIT. Don't be silly. I think it would be much better if someone kept a close watch on you, just in case you have a funny turn in the night. It could affect you later you know, being hit on your head.

THOMAS. But it's quite unfair to ask George to do such a thing.

GEORGE. I don't mind, it could be fun. I've never looked after anyone before. I can sit in the chair and read my book. I never sleep at night anyway, only ever drop off when the birds start singing. They're fresh sheets as well, I only washed them the other day.

THOMAS. Well, I don't know...

GEORGE. Go on, Mr Thomas.

THOMAS. No, please, Cyril.

GEORGE. Cyril. Go on, you won't be any trouble and Brenda's right: you could go a bit funny later on, you never know.

THOMAS. Well, if you're sure you don't mind.

GEORGE. Of course I don't.

THOMAS. I suppose it would be for the best.

TEBBIT. Of course it is.

THOMAS. Oh alright then. Just for tonight though, I shall be alright by tomorrow. Thank you, George. Thank you very much indeed.

GEORGE. Think nothing of it.

TEBBIT. It's his pleasure, isn't it, George?

GEORGE. Yes, it's my pleasure, Cyril.

THOMAS. Thank you.

GEORGE. You're welcome.

Pause.

TEBBIT. Well, at least one good thing has come out of this; we've all got to know each other a bit better.

GEORGE. That's true.

TEBBIT. They do say a crisis brings people closer together. Just goes to show there's a lot of truth in that doesn't it, George?

GEORGE. Yeah.

THOMAS. Do you know, at the last place I lived there were six of us all in the same house and I never knew any of their names. Two years I stayed there. I remember the house was always very quiet. I used to walk about on my tiptoes day and night. It wasn't because I had to, I just felt I should. Strange isn't it?

TEBBIT. Very. I don't know how you could stick it.

THOMAS. It wasn't that bad, just a bit lonely at times, that's all.

TEBBIT. Still, you're amongst friends now.

THOMAS. Yes, this is much more pleasant. (*Flinches and rubs his side.*) Oh dear.

TEBBIT. Are you alright, Cyril?

THOMAS. Just a slight pain in my side.

TEBBIT. Come on. It's time you were in bed.

THOMAS. Oh no. I'm fine, honestly.

TEBBIT. No you're not, you're in pain. It would be much better for you if you got into bed.

THOMAS. But I'm enjoying our little chat.

TEBBIT. Just because you're getting into bed it doesn't mean you have to keep your mouth shut does it? Come on, George, help me get him sorted.

GEORGE. Righty-oh. (*They go through the process of getting* THOMAS *into bed.*) It's quite comfy but there's a spring sticking out somewhere near the bottom, so you watch your feet.

TEBBIT. Is there?

GEORGE. Yeah.

TEBBIT. How long has it been like that?

GEORGE. Just a couple of weeks.

TEBBIT. Why didn't you tell me about it?

GEORGE. I didn't think it was important.

TEBBIT. Well I think the comfort of my residents is very important. You should have reported it to me the moment it started poking through the material. Remind me in the morning to order a new mattress from the Co-op. Now, are you comfy, Cyril?

THOMAS. I'm as snug as a bug in a rug.

TEBBIT. Oh I am pleased.

GEORGE. I always thought it was slug.

TEBBIT. I beg your pardon, George?

GEORGE. I always thought it was snug as a slug in a rug, but it's not is it, it's bug.

TEBBIT. Well of course it's bug, how can a slug look snug? (*Laughs.*) Honestly, Cyril, these young people.

GEORGE. Well I know now, don't I?

TEBBIT. You are silly, George.

GEORGE (*grins*). I know,

TEBBIT (*sits*). Could you get me another brandy please?

GEORGE. Course. Do you want one, Cyril?

THOMAS. Not for me, thank you.

GEORGE. Can I have another one?

TEBBIT. Of course you can, no need to ask.

GEORGE. Cheers. (*Pours out the drinks, then sits on the floor.*)

TEBBIT. You alright, Cyril?

THOMAS. Perfect.

TEBBIT. You look very contented. Doesn't he look contented, George?

GEORGE. Very.

THOMAS. 'Weary with toil, I haste me to my bed,
The dear repose for limbs with travel tired;
But then begins a journey in my head,
To work my mind, when body's work's expir'd.'
Shakespeare.

TEBBIT. Oh how very cultured.

GEORGE. I can never understand him.

TEBBIT. Well I don't think you have to really, it just sounds pretty, doesn't it.

THOMAS. I want you to know that I'm going to close my eyes for a few moments. I'm not going to sleep, I just want to rest my eyes, so please carry on chatting.

TEBBIT. Are you sure?

THOMAS. Quite sure. It's very soothing listening to you talk.

TEBBIT. I'm not going to stay much longer anyway, I'm quite worn out. I've never known an evening like it.

GEORGE. It's been a long day hasn't it?

TEBBIT. Very.

Pause.

How's your sister keeping?

GEORGE. Oh, she's fine thank you.

TEBBIT. Has she got any children?

GEORGE. No. I don't think they want any yet.

TEBBIT. Want to wait a while do they?

GEORGE. I think so, yes.

Pause.

TEBBIT. I like Brighton.

GEORGE. So do I.

TEBBIT. Nice, isn't it?

GEORGE. Lovely.

TEBBIT. I think I like Hastings better though, on account of the castle.

GEORGE. I've never been to Hastings.

TEBBIT. Oh you should try and go some time, it's lovely.

GEORGE. Maybe we could go together, have a day out.

TEBBIT. Yes. We could go by train and fetch a picnic.

GEORGE. I'd like that.

TEBBIT. Of course it's much better to go for a couple of days. you can take everything in at a more relaxing pace.

GEORGE. Yeah, I suppose you could.

TEBBIT. Book into a nice little hotel overlooking the sea. I've always wanted to do that.

GEORGE. We should do it then, in the summer.

TEBBIT. I haven't had a holiday since 1952.

GEORGE. It'd do you good then.

TEBBIT. We could get a double room.

GEORGE. Could we?

TEBBIT. Oh yeah, it'd be cheaper than two singles.

GEORGE. I suppose it would.

TEBBIT. Have a nice big double bed to frolick about on. (*She goes and checks on* THOMAS.) Cyril? Cyril? Aaahh, he's fast asleep, poor love.

GEORGE. He dropped off quick.

TEBBIT. So would you if you'd been hit on the head with a brick. (*Sits.*)

Pause.

GEORGE. You're a very sophisticated woman, Brenda.

TEBBIT. Oh, George, you do say the nicest things.

GEORGE. I mean it.

TEBBIT. I really can't understand why you haven't got a girlfriend, you've got such lovely qualities.

GEORGE. That's because I feel comfortable with you, I can be myself.

TEBBIT. Maybe you see me as a mother figure.

GEORGE. I don't think so.

TEBBIT. What do you see me as then?

GEORGE. I don't know, a lady I suppose, a woman.

TEBBIT. Oh you smooth-talker, you. Come over here and give us a kiss.

GEORGE. Pardon?

TEBBIT. Don't you want to?

GEORGE. Wouldn't you mind?

TEBBIT. I've been wanting one all night.

GEORGE. What, off me?

TEBBIT. Well I don't want my lipstick smudged by four eyes over there do I? Come on, George, what are you frightened of?

GEORGE. I'm not frightened.

TEBBIT. Come over here then.

GEORGE (*makes his way over to her on his knees*). What if Mr Thomas wakes up?

TEBBIT. He'll be asleep for hours yet.

GEORGE i*s kneeling in front of her and she runs her fingers through his hair.*

You're very sexual you know, George.

GEORGE. Am I?

TEBBIT. Oh yes. There's definitely something of the Humphrey Bogart in you.

GEORGE. Really?

TEBBIT. And in my younger days I was told I was like a taller Lauren Bacall. I'm also a bit more filled out than her but I don't like to brag.

She grabs him and kisses him quite violently. After a few seconds, we hear a loud knock coming from the front door downstairs.

GEORGE. What was that?

TEBBIT (*pissed off*). Well what do you think it was?

GEORGE. Sounds like someone knocking on the front door.

TEBBIT. Ten out of ten.

More knocks.

GEORGE. Shall I answer it?

TEBBIT. You'd better, otherwise Mr Thomas might wake up.

GEORGE (*gets up*). Right.

TEBBIT. And whoever it is, try and get rid of them, I was just beginning to enjoy myself.

GEORGE. Yeah, so was I. (*Exits*.)

TEBBIT *goes over to* THOMAS, *takes his glasses off and puts them on the side table. She goes to the mirror, checks her hair, then pours herself another brandy. We hear some commotion outside then* GEORGE *enters holding up a very drunk* WEAVER.

WEAVER. Georgy-porgy pudding and pie...

TEBBIT. Bloody hell!

WEAVER. Hello, Brenda, my darling.

TEBBIT. What are you doing here?

WEAVER (*falls into the chair*). Me and Gordon thought we'd come and visit you, make up for your lost evening. I brought some gin.

TEBBIT. Is Gordon here as well?

GEORGE. He's collapsed in the passage downstairs.

TEBBIT. Collapsed?

GEORGE. Well he sort of went all floppy, then slid down the wall. I think he's had a few too many.

WEAVER. He's had the same amount as me, he just can't hold it, the fucking idiot.

TEBBIT. We'll have less of that talk, thank you very much.

WEAVER. Sorry, darling, I forgot you was here.

GEORGE. What are we gonna do about Gordon?

TEBBIT. Well, we can't just leave him down there, you'll have to help him upstairs.

GEORGE. I can't manage him on my own and Weaver's not much help at the moment.

WEAVER. I'm quite capable of carrying that skinny tit up a flight of stairs.

TEBBIT. You stay where you are, me and George'll get him.

WEAVER (*notes* THOMAS). Who's that?

TEBBIT. That is Mr Thomas.

WEAVER. What, that bloke from earlier?

TEBBIT. Yes.

WEAVER. What's he doing in George's bed? You three been playing naughty games?

GEORGE. Don't be stupid.

TEBBIT. We thought it best that he stayed up here for the night so that George could keep an eye on him.

WEAVER. Did he tell you what happened to him?

TEBBIT. Partly, yes.

WEAVER. What did he say?

TEBBIT. I really don't think that's any of your business.

WEAVER. Did he tell you anything, George?

TEBBIT. Mr Thomas spoke to me in private.

WEAVER. Is he going to the police?

TEBBIT. At the moment he doesn't want to but I'm hoping to change his mind.

WEAVER. I wouldn't take any notice of what he told you. He looks a bit shifty to me.

TEBBIT. I can assure you he is not shifty.

WEAVER. Well what did he tell you then?

TEBBIT. Please, Mr Weaver...

WEAVER. I mean, does he know who did it to him, because if he does I'm quite willing to sort them out for him. It's out of order ain't it, he's only a little bloke.

TEBBIT. That's very kind of you but Mr Thomas only knew the culprit by sight. Now we can't stand here chatting all night, we'd better go and fetch Gordon. Weaver, would you keep an eye on Mr Thomas for me, he had a knock on his head you see, so he might have a funny turn.

WEAVER. Certainly. I may be pissed out of my brain but I'm in total control of me whereabouts.

TEBBIT. Right. Come on, George, let's do our duty.

GEORGE. We won't be a minute.

They both exit.

WEAVER *looks at* THOMAS. *He gets up and goes over to him. He gives him a little dig and* THOMAS *stirs.* WEAVER *then gets a pillow from the bed and puts it over* THOMAS*'s head. As he is suffocating* THOMAS *there are kicks and struggles from under the bedclothes.* WEAVER *finds this sexually exciting and starts to make fuck noises. There are a few more kicks until* THOMAS *is dead. After a few seconds* WEAVER *stops and puts the pillow back in its original place. He walks away, spots something is wrong, picks up the eyeglasses and puts them back on* THOMAS. *He takes a bottle of gin from his pocket, drinks from it then sits back in the chair. After a few moments* GEORGE *and* TEBBIT *return carrying* GORDON.

GORDON (*very drunk*). I can assure you I'm perfectly alright.

TEBBIT. Weaver, would you mind if we put Mr Davis in the chair?

WEAVER (*gets up*). Be my guest, I don't mind sitting on the floor, there's no boils on my bum.

GORDON (*falls into chair*). I'm so sorry, Mrs Tebbit, I don't make a habit of this sort of thing.

TEBBIT. I'm sure you don't, you've just had a few too many that's all.

WEAVER. Bollocks! He's always pissed, him, ain't he, George?

GEORGE. Not always, no.

WEAVER. Yes he is. He can't hold it. He only had four whiskys and that was it, splattered.

TEBBIT. I'm really not interested.

GEORGE. You shouldn't have come back here you know, not at this time of night.

WEAVER. Brenda don't mind, do you, Brenda?

TEBBIT. I do actually, but there's not a lot I can do about it now.

WEAVER (*gets up*). Oh well, if that's how you feel, I'll be off.

GEORGE. Don't be silly.

WEAVER. No, no, I insist. You're quite right, Brenda, I took a liberty and I'm sorry. I'm quite capable of getting myself home unlike Bette Davis there. I think you should put him up for the night but I'm fine, ain't I.

TEBBIT. Well if you're sure you don't mind. I mean it's bad enough that George has to look after Mr Thomas.

WEAVER. Oh yeah, of course.

GEORGE. I wonder if he's alright. (*Goes over to* THOMAS.)

WEAVER. He's fine, I just looked at him, sleeping like a baby he is.

GEORGE. He's still got his glasses on.

TEBBIT. That's funny…

GEORGE. Shall I take them off him?

TEBBIT. You'd better, otherwise he might turn over in the night and hurt himself.

WEAVER. Maybe he always wears them in bed to see his dreams better.

TEBBIT. Oh, Weaver, you are funny.

GEORGE (*lifts* THOMAS*'s head and removes the glasses*). Blimey, he's out for the count.

TEBBIT (*smoothes the blankets*). He's in another world.

WEAVER. Yeah well, don't fiddle about with him you'll wake him up.

TEBBIT. He's right, George, come away now. Oh dear, it looks like Mr Davis has dropped off as well.

WEAVER. Well I'm on my way, so you've no worries there.

TEBBIT. You can stay if you like, you can have Mr Thomas's bed.

WEAVER. No, you're alright. I could do with the walk, it might sober me up. Will you be alright with Gordon, George?

GEORGE. How do you mean?

WEAVER. Well you know, in case he has one of his turns.

GEORGE. What turns?

WEAVER. Ain't you ever seen him throw a wobbly?

GEORGE. No.

WEAVER. Oh. Perhaps he only does it with me, I don't think he likes me very much.

TEBBIT. Why, what does he do?

WEAVER. Nothing much, just gets a bit violent, that's all. It's mainly talk though, I've never actually seen him hit anyone. He can never remember anything about it the next day, he sort of blacks out.

TEBBIT. Oh dear, I don't like the sound of that.

WEAVER. I'm sure he'll be alright though. Look at him, he's out for the night.

TEBBIT. I hope so.

WEAVER. Now don't you worry yourself about it. He won't get up to anything, he's in no state to.

GEORGE. Blimey, you learn something new every day. Mind you, only this morning he was going on about how he screams all the time. He sits on his own in his flat and screams.

TEBBIT. Poor thing, he don't sound right in the head.

WEAVER. If you want me to stay, I will.

TEBBIT. No, you get off home to bed.

WEAVER. Wish I'd never said anything now. I don't want you to worry.

GEORGE. We're not worried; he won't do anything. I'm glad you told us about him though.

WEAVER. Right, I'll be off. Oh – (*Takes the gin out of his pocket.*) you might as well have this, I bought it for you anyway.

TEBBIT. Thank you, Weaver.

WEAVER. I took a couple of swigs, just to keep the cold out on the way over.

TEBBIT. That's perfectly alright.

WEAVER. I'll pop up in the morning, just to see if everything's alright.

GEORGE. Yeah. See you then.

TEBBIT. Mind how you go now.

WEAVER. Right. Cheerio then. (*Exits.*)

GEORGE (*gets an overcoat and covers* GORDON). Ain't that funny about old Gordon, he just don't seem the type.

TEBBIT. You can't judge a book by its cover, George.

GEORGE. That's true.

Pause.

TEBBIT. Well, I think I'd better be getting to my bed now.

GEORGE. Oh. Right.

TEBBIT. It's a pity about this evening, we were just beginning to get to know each other better.

GEORGE. Yeah. I know.

Pause.

TEBBIT. Would you be a gentleman and walk me to my room?

GEORGE. I'd be delighted.

TEBBIT. And you might like to come in for a nightcap, I've got the gin.

GEORGE. I can't stay too long though, can I.

TEBBIT. Oh no, you've got patients to look after.

GEORGE. Right then.

TEBBIT. Right then. (*They exit and close the door.*)

The sound of the door closing wakes GORDON. *He looks around confused. He looks at the bed and staggers out of the chair. He sits on the end of the bed and takes off his shoes. He moves* THOMAS *across the bed.*

GORDON. Come on, old chap, make way for the rest of the troops. (*Gets in the bed not facing* THOMAS.) I hope you don't mind, but there's enough room for three in here, never mind two.

Pause.

You know, I do so hate sleeping in a chair don't you? It's most unpleasant. You wake up as stiff as a corpse in the morning.

Blackout.

The End.

www.nickhernbooks.co.uk

facebook.com/nickhernbooks

twitter.com/nickhernbooks